The desert and the city

A Lenten journey with Christ

Ray Simpson

kevin
mayhew

First published in 2005 by

KEVIN MAYHEW LTD
Buxhall, Stowmarket, Suffolk, IP14 3BW
E-mail: info@kevinmayhewltd.com
Web: www.kevinmayhew.com

9 8 7 6 5 4 3 2 1 0

ISBN 1 84417 485 9
Catalogue No 1500857

Cover illustration by Angela Palfrey
Cover design by Angela Selfe
Typesetting by Richard Weaver

Printed in Great Britain

CONTENTS

About the author

Ray Simpson is a co-founder of the worldwide Community of Aidan and Hilda and is its first guardian. He is a priest and pastor in the Christian Church, and a well-known author. He lives on The Holy Island of Lindisfarne, near to the Community's Retreat and Guest House, The Open Gate, Holy Island, Berwick Upon Tweed, TD15 2SD, UK.

Also by Ray Simpson:

Celtic Daily Light: a spiritual journey throughout the year
Church of the Isles: a prophetic strategy for renewal
Exploring Celtic Spirituality: historic roots for our future
A Pilgrim Way: a new Celtic monasticism for everyday people
Prayer Rhythms for Busy People: a pocket companion
Let dreams come true: An Advent course

The Celtic Prayer Book is published in four volumes:

Volume One
Prayer Rhythms: fourfold patterns for each day and season

Volume Two
Saints of the Isles: a year of feasts

Volume Three
Healing the Land: natural seasons, sacraments and special services

Volume Four
Great Celtic Christians: alternative worship

INTRODUCTION

Those who honour God in the world's great Faiths set aside certain periods when they refocus their lives on what is eternally important. The chief period for Muslims is Ramadan and for Christians Lent. Judaism has given us the story of the journey through the desert to the Promised Land as a powerful image of life's journey – both outwardly in time and space and inwardly in the deeps of the spirit.

Some followers of these Faiths extricated themselves from immediate preoccupations and went alone into a desert. In early Christian centuries thousands flocked into the deserts of the Middle East in order to live lives of God-filled simplicity. They fired the imagination of British and Irish people, who then chose deserts of their own – isolated places in which they could devote themselves to prayer and gain spiritual strength and wisdom. An equivalent word to 'desert' used in many English translations of the Bible is the word 'wilderness', which literally means 'the place of wild deer' – and it was in such places that many Celtic and Saxon saints made their homes.

However, a desert experience need not necessarily take place in a desert (or in a wilderness) but can also take place in a busy town or city, because it is essentially an inner experience of the soul. Many ordinary people who have done extraordinary things for God often go through some kind of desert experience. One of the sermons of John Wesley, the eighteenth century evangelist and founder of Methodism, was entitled 'The Wilderness State' and concerned what medieval saints called 'the dark night of the soul'.

What these saints tell us is that it is in such 'desert' experiences that we fight our greatest spiritual battles. Jesus himself chose to spend six weeks in a physical desert of temptation before he began his public ministry. But his greatest test came later, in the city of Jerusalem, where he was led into a spiritual desert of treachery, trial, abandonment and death. Yet it was through his struggle both in the desert and the city that he gained the ultimate victory. There was no other way.

The great religions call us to seasons of self-discipline and reflection which are like a pilgrimage into a desert. The idea of going into a desert has taken such root that, now, many people who cannot physically leave home and travel to a desert nevertheless make an inner desert journey.

The season of Lent – the 40 days (excluding Sundays) before the Easter celebration of Christ's resurrection – is an opportunity to walk with Christ through his desert – not just the wilderness of Judaea, but the city of Jerusalem, where he was tried and tested, and outside which he died. By walking with him we shall confront our own weaknesses and strengths, as well as his. Jesus was always vulnerable, from his birth in a stable to his death on a cross, and we are called to follow him in his vulnerability.

Seekers and Christians learn about Christ's resurrection in courses such as *Alpha*, and go on to learn about God's Holy Spirit. These are the 'highs' of Christianity. But Lent takes us to the 'lows', through the valleys we must traverse before we reach the mountain top. It takes us into humdrum places of weakness, questioning and struggle – places where we are at our most vulnerable, places of testing, sorrow, anger and pain. We will find that Christ also traversed these places and, in our hearts, we will accompany him. As we do so, we will learn that he also accompanies us in our heartache valleys, and leads us to fresh horizons.

If we just 'do the course' for 90 minutes once a week with a group, we will miss its secret. We need to prepare ourselves inwardly and privately too, so that we can share in Christ's journey in our thoughts through all the days of Lent. How may we create space for this? By giving something up. Some people give up chocolate or a bad habit. Why not give up something that robs us of time, so that we can dedicate the time saved to quiet reflection? This 'something' could be a meal, a TV 'soap' or an activity – you will know what is appropriate for you. Then some time in the week before each session can be given to reflection on the Bible passage assigned to the session. If this is done, the effect of the course on the participants' lives will be so much greater, and so much more beneficial.

RAY SIMPSON
Lindisfarne Retreat - www.aidan.org.uk

NOTES FOR LEADERS

Each session of the course usually has the following structure:

Starter   Getting things going
Contemplation   A visual focus
Scripture   Studying the passage for the week
Sifting   Following up the study
Steps   Actions as well as words
Surrender   A closing act of dedication

A list of things is provided at the beginning of the session notes, which you (as leader) need to bring or prepare for the session. Be prepared, so that the session can run smoothly. Note that for Week Five you will need to know something about Bethany, Mary, Martha and Lazarus. Look them up in a Bible Dictionary. There are also several musical items which will need to be provided – recordings to listen to (and something to play them on) or words to sing and perhaps an instrument to play the tune. It is essential, also, that you have done a thorough study of the set Bible passage beforehand so that you can guide the discussion and make an effective contribution to it.

You may wish to delegate some of the subsections to other members of the group.

Group members will need to know which Bible passage to study before the next meeting.

Any version of the Bible could be used, but the inclusion of modern versions such as 'The Street Bible', 'The Message' or 'The Dramatised Bible' might be particularly helpful (alongside more traditional versions, of course).

A decision will have to be made at, or before, the beginning of the course about how each session will end – *Refreshments, conversation or silence?*

THE DESERT OF TESTING

Preparations

Remember to ask group members to prepare for this session by studying Matthew 4:1-11 beforehand at home, so that they can share their thoughts on the passage with the rest of the group during the session. They also need to bring Bibles with them to every session.

Prepare sand in a large tray or on a polythene sheet. Make a footprint in the sand. You will also need a cross, a bag of stones and a CD of 'Lawrence of Arabia' music; also the music and words of the song, 'All to Jesus I surrender', or the hymn, 'All for Jesus – all for Jesus', or something with a similar theme.

Starter

Ask group members to write down things which the word 'desert' brings to their minds. Ask them to share their findings.

Contemplation

Place the sand tray (with footprint) where everyone can see it clearly. Play the 'Lawrence of Arabia' music quietly in the background.

Reader   Those who have hungered for God in the past often learned to refocus their lives on God by extricating themselves from their immediate preoccupations and going alone into the desert. Jesus himself did this. During Lent God can lead *us* into the desert too.

This week we will try and journey with Jesus into his desert of testing. In this way he prepared himself for his three-year-long public mission, which led to the momentous final week of his life.

> For two minutes we shall try to imagine that this is Jesus' footprint in the sand and think of him spending 40 days and nights fasting in the desert.

Towards the end of the two minutes let the music fade away.

Scripture

Matthew 4:1-11

Leader Jesus struggled in the desert. He experienced confusion. Two voices were speaking inside him. Sometimes one seemed more reasonable than the other, but Jesus asked himself if the motivation of this voice was absolutely pure. He may not have been sure at first what was God's will, but after checking out the motivations, he gained a settled conviction as to what was right.

Ask someone to read the passage aloud.

The group then share their thoughts on the passage and discuss what they learned from their private studies earlier in the week.

Leader Jesus later reflected on these 40 days in the desert and passed on what happened to his disciples. He summarised three main temptations. The first one was to satisfy his own hunger by turning stones into bread. How did he reject this temptation?

　　　　What does it mean to 'live by bread alone'? What does it mean to live by every word that comes from the mouth of God? Is it the same as feeding our spirits as well as our bodies? Did it mean that to Jesus? (see John 4:31-34).

　　　　The second temptation was to throw himself down from the Temple and rely on God to keep him safe. What did this temptation mean? How did Jesus reject it?

　　　　Have you ever put God to the test by asking him to work a miracle to prove his existence? How else might this temptation apply to us?

The third temptation was to win the world by worshipping the devil. How did Jesus reject this temptation? In what ways might we be tempted to promote our own interests and become a success in life by 'worshipping the devil'?

Sifting

Leader   Are our temptations different from Jesus', or are they essentially the same?

How did Jesus manage to fend off the tempter? Was it easier or harder for him than it is for us? Can we learn anything from him about this?

Steps

Place a cross on the sand. Give each person a few stones.

Leader   Imagine Jesus called you to follow him as he goes on his mission, and that the stones represent 'excess baggage' in your life which would prevent you from going with him (including habits, attitudes, weaknesses which you would be reluctant to leave behind). Decide what the stones represent and then place them by the cross and return to your seat in silence.

Surrender

Invite any who wish to share with the group what their stones represent. Others may wish to keep their thoughts to themselves.

All may sit or kneel in an act of surrender as they sing: 'All to Jesus I surrender' *or* 'All for Jesus – all for Jesus'.

There may be silence or free prayer, or the following may be said:

Reader Jesus, you were driven into the wilderness by the searching Spirit:

All Strip from us what is not of you.

Reader You were alone, without comfort or food:

All Help us to rely on you alone.

Reader Though tested by the Evil One you clung to no falsehood:

All Break in us the hold of power and pride.

Reader You followed to the end the way of the cross:

All Strengthen *us* to stay true to the end.

Reader At this time of Christ's testings and trials:

All Let us remain faithful to him.

Reader Christ showed us the way:

All Give us the courage to follow in his footsteps.

Let each person in turn say to the one on their right:

> May you walk in the steps of Christ this week
> and become more aware of his thoughts.

There may be refreshments, conversation or silence.

Ask the group members to study **Matthew 21:1-11** *at home in preparation for the next session.*

THE WAY OF MEEKNESS

Preparations

Provide a picture of Jesus on a donkey, enough palm crosses for the group, or paper and scissors for them to make their own crosses or 'palm leaves'. Have a CD of Passion music by composers such as Bach, Fauré, Lloyd Webber or Stainer.

Starter

Ask the group what the word 'meek' means to them. Discuss.

Then ask them what they think Jesus meant when he said: 'The meek shall inherit the earth'.

Contemplation

Place the picture of Jesus on a donkey where everyone can see it.

Leader   Contemplate this picture and listen to these words from two well-known hymns, noting the contrasts:

Ride on, ride on in majesty!
Hark, all the tribes 'Hosanna' cry;
thine humble beast pursues his road
with palms and scattered garments strowed.

Ride on, ride on in majesty!
In lowly pomp ride on to die;
bow thy meek head to mortal pain,
then take, O God, thy power, and reign.

(*Henry Hart Milman, 1791-1868*)

Sometimes they strew his way,
and his sweet praises sing;
resounding all the day
hosannas to their King;
then 'Crucify!' is all their breath,
and for his death
they thirst and cry.   (*Samuel Crossman, 1624-84*)

Leader   Do you think meekness and majesty are compatible with
each other?

Doesn't meekness make people vulnerable to bullies?
Was Jesus vulnerable in that way?

Scripture

Matthew 21:1-11

Ask someone to read the passage aloud.

Ask the group to share the results of their private studies of this passage.

Leader   Christ entered his capital city, where he knew he would
be roughed up, 'gentle and riding on a donkey' (Zechariah
9:9, Matthew 21:5).

Many of his fellow citizens regarded him as their
uncrowned king. Christians believe that he 'came down
from the heights of heaven' for us. Yet he chose to make
his way through the crowds, not as a VIP on a military
horse, but on the most menial of everyday creatures, a
mule.

Jesus' cousin, John, who led a mass reform movement,
profiled Jesus as 'the Lamb of God' (John 1:29,36). Those
who observed Jesus' stance when he was dragged before
officials, who could either free him or condemn him to
death, said that he was silent (see Matthew 26:63; 27:12-
14; Mark 14:61; 15:5; Luke 23:9; John 19:9). In this he
reminds us of the prophecy of Isaiah 53:7. Yet he was not
weak; he endured torture with great courage.

13

Sifting

Leader   When the Apostle Paul listed 'gentleness' as one of the nine fruits of God's Spirit (Galatians 5:23) he used the word *praotes*. This word overflows with meanings; it is far removed from some current images of gentleness as unreasonable sweetness, powerless passivity, or timidity. The Philosopher, Plato, considered gentleness to be 'the cement of society'. Aristotle defined it as the mean between being too angry and never becoming angry: the gentle person expresses anger for the right reason and duration, and in the right way. It is the characteristic needed when exercising discipline (Galatians 6:1), facing opposition (2 Timothy 2:25), and opening ourselves to hearing God's Word without pride (James 1:21).

In twos or threes give examples from your own or someone else's experience of 'strong gentleness' that reflects a little of this quality in Jesus.

Leader   Do we need to redefine our original ideas of meekness? Are there any better words we could use instead of meekness?

Does all this tell us any more about the meaning of Jesus' beatitude: 'Blessed are the meek, for they shall inherit the earth'?

Steps

Distribute 'palm crosses' or ask each member of the group to cut out their own 'palm crosses' or palm leaves and then lay them before the picture of Jesus.

Leader   We bring these palm leaves as signs of our dedication to Jesus, 'spreading ourselves before him, not scattering olive branches or garments or palms, but spreading ourselves before him as best we can, with him in our souls' (Words of St Andrew of Crete).

Surrender

Listen to recorded Passion music of Bach, Fauré, Lloyd Webber, Stainer's 'God so loved the world' *or the hymn* 'O sacred head sore wounded'.

Reader 'Take my yoke upon you and learn from me, for I am gentle and humble in heart, and you will find rest for your souls' (Matthew 11:29).

He who created us comes willingly to suffer for us.

All Let us spread our resolves before him like palm leaves.

Reader The Almighty comes to us as one who is gentle and lowly of heart.

All Let us don clothes for him of humility and praise.

Reader The spirit is willing but the flesh is weak.

All Let us walk with the strong but gentle Christ through his last days on this earth. Amen.

There may be refreshments, conversation or silence.

Ask the group members to study **Luke 19:41-44** *at home in preparation for the next session.*

THE CITY OF SADNESS

Preparations

You will need an ikon or a picture of Jesus weeping; sheets of paper, pencils, a bowl of stones, felt tips with which to write on the stones and a CD of plaintive bagpipe music or Lloyd Webber's 'Pie Jesu'; the words and music of 'My song is love unknown'.

Starter

Leader   What do you think Jesus meant when he said, 'Happy are those who mourn, for they shall be comforted'?

Contemplation

Place a picture of a sad or weeping Christ where all can see it.
Play some plaintive bagpipe music or Lloyd Webber's 'Pie Jesu'.

Leader   As you look at this picture and listen to this music, think why The City of Jerusalem which Jesus loved made him so sad and even moved him to tears.

Ask someone to read Matthew 23:37.

Leader   Think what things in the modern world make *you* sad – not personal things but things in the wider community. Ask God to keep you sensitive to the world's wrongs and not to let you become hardened by them so that you take them for granted and don't try to do anything about them.

Scripture

Luke 19:41-44

Ask someone to read the passage aloud.

Ask the group members to share the thoughts prompted by their study of this passage in preparation for this session.

Leader   Why did Jesus weep for Jerusalem?

What would make him weep in *our* day?

What are the things that make for peace – then and now?

Sifting

Leader   Jerusalem was not just a city of stone, but a city of stony hearts. They had not responded to Jesus' mission of love. Has the moral teaching, compassionate example, and self-sacrifice of Jesus Christ had a softening influence on human civilisation over the centuries? Has Jesus Christ had a softening influence on you?

Have you been hardened in any way by your life experience?

These are not easy questions; try to give honest answers. In order to help you answer the personal questions, I want you to make your own brief life charts.

Distribute pencils and sheets of paper around the group.

Ask group members to divide their page into six sections horizontally, and to number the sections as follows:

1 Child   2 Adolescent   3 Student/Starting work

4 Early adult   5 Relationships   6 Losses/Changes

Ask them to note down the memory of something in each section which either (a) made them more compassionate; or (b) made them harder.

After about five or ten minutes ask them to share some of their memories in twos.

Steps

Leader   Just saying a confession in church may not always be enough to express, or even arouse, our feelings of penitence. The meaning of the words has to work its way down from our heads into our hearts.

Catholic Christians use a Rosary to recall the 'sorrowful mysteries' in the heart of Mary prompted by events in the life of Jesus. (*If anyone in the group uses a Rosary they could explain it to those who aren't familiar with it.*)

Now I invite you to take some stones from this bowl and use them to reflect on the things in the world that make you sad and the things which tend to harden your hearts. Write some of these things on the stones and then place them by the picture of Jesus.

Surrender

Leader   Would any of you like to share with the group what you have written on your stones?

Now let us sit or kneel in silence as we surrender our hearts to Jesus and then say (or sing) the hymn: 'My song is love unknown'.

Reader   We draw aside at the end of the day (*or in the midst of the day*).
We weep for the hungry and poor,
the children mistreated, those broken by force
and the maimed who can't finish their course.

All   We plead for your justice to fill all the lands
as the waters cover the sands.

Reader   We pray against cruelty, hatred and pain,
against pride and greed for gain.
We pray for the homeless and victims of war,
the strangers to love at the door.

All   We plead for your justice to fill all the lands
as the waters cover the sands.   *Andrew Dick*

18

Leader   God of the tears,

All   give us tears for your people.

Leader   God who mothers us,

All   draw us into your arms.

Leader   God who is one,

All   make us one with you.

There may be refreshments, conversation or silence.

Ask the group members to study **Matthew 21:12-17** *at home in preparation for the next session.*

Week Four

THE PLACE OF ANGER

Preparations

You will need a picture of Jesus 'cleansing the Temple', and a bag of coins; also a CD of 'Jesus Christ Superstar' or 'Olivet to Calvary'. Have pencils and paper ready for making lists. Choose a hymn for the 'Surrender' section and have the words and music ready.

Starter

Ask the group to think of times when they were angry. Ask them to list words which describe how people might feel after *they've been angry.*

Contemplation

Place a picture of Christ in the Temple where everyone can see it. Empty a bag of coins in front of it and leave the empty bag there too.

Leader   Let us spend a minute or two looking at the picture of Jesus cleansing the Temple, while we listen to music inspired by this story. (*Say which piece you are going to play – either from* 'Jesus Christ Superstar' *or from* 'Olivet to Calvary'.)

Allow a short time of silence after the music has faded, then bring the contemplation to a close with a short prayer such as the following:

Leader   Lord, cleanse our Temples – our places of worship – that they may be places of welcome, beauty, truth and love.
     Lord, cleanse the Temples of our hearts – that they may be full of goodness, kindness and openness to others and we may know how to worship you in spirit and in truth. In the name of Jesus Christ. Amen.

Scripture

Matthew 21:12-17

Ask someone to read the passage aloud.

Ask the group to share the results of their private study of this passage.

Leader   There seems to be no doubt that Jesus was angry on this occasion. What made him so angry? Make a list of reasons (see also Mark 11:17).

It is also clear that Jesus expressed his anger violently in the Temple. What forms did his violence take? In what way was it effective – (a) there and then (*see verses 14-16);* (b) in the longer term?

What do you think Jesus meant to achieve by his actions in the Temple?

Sifting

Leader   The cause Jesus demonstrated for was that people of every background and race should have a welcoming access to God in the public place of worship.

How far do our churches cater for and welcome visitors – both at worship and at other times? Are they open to any who care to come in? If so, do they offer the place and opportunity for undisturbed prayer, or for private conversation, or for something to eat and drink?

How welcoming are our churches to people of other faith communities?

How welcoming are our churches to children – in worship and at other times?

Steps

Gather up the coins and put them in the bag. Remove the picture and replace it with a simple cross.

Leader Because Jesus died on a cross he died with outstretched arms – as if welcoming and embracing the whole world. It also gave extra force to his words: 'Father, forgive them for they know not what they do.'

The early Christians in Britain and Ireland often prayed with their arms stretched out in the shape of a cross. It may not be a practice which is familiar to you, but let's try it now. Find enough space so that you can stretch out your arms without touching anybody or anything else. Note how it feels.

Think of the negative feelings first – you may feel embarrassed or ridiculous. You get the idea that someone is laughing at you. Worse still you may feel exposed and vulnerable, just as Jesus was on the cross.

Now think of the positive feelings – you are more open and free, warm and welcoming – the kind of feelings you get when you are greeting a friend, especially one you haven't seen for a long time, or rejoicing at the return of a lost child, or celebrating a great achievement. Jesus may have had positive feelings on the cross too, when he said, 'It is finished!' (John 19:30) and cried out with a loud voice, 'Father, into your hands I commend my spirit' (Luke 23:46).

After a short moment of quiet ask the group to relax their arms and return to their seats.

Surrender

Sing a hymn about Jesus on the cross, e.g. 'When I survey the wondrous cross', 'Lift high the cross', 'There is a green hill far away'. *There are many more.*

Say the words of either the following prayer or the following hymn together as an act of surrender to God's love in Christ:

Either   O Christ, you were put to death by cruel people
           who nailed your arms to a cross;
       yet long before, you stretched out your arms
           in love to all.
       May your way be our way.
       May we, too, stretch out our arms in love to all.

or   O dearest Lord, thy sacred head
           with thorns was pierced for me.
       O pour thy blessing on my head,
           that I may think for thee.

       O dearest Lord, thy sacred hands
           with nails were pierced for me.
       O shed thy blessing on my hands,
           that they may work for thee.

       O dearest Lord, thy sacred feet
           with nails were pierced for me.
       O pour thy blessing on my feet,
           that they may follow thee.

       O dearest Lord, thy sacred heart
           with spear was pierced for me.
       O pour thy spirit in my heart,
           that I may live for thee.

(Father Andrew [H. E. Hardy], 1869-1946)

© *Mowbray/Cassell plc. an imprint of Continuum Int. Publishing Group,*
The Tower Building, 11 York Road, London, SE1 7NX

There may be refreshments, conversation or silence.

*Ask the group members to study **John 12:1-8** at home in preparation for the next session.*

Week Five

THE HOUSE OF HOSPITALITY

Preparations

Find a picture of Bethany or a map with Bethany on it and place it with a jar of scented oil, and a candle or incense ready to be lit, on a table covered with a beautiful cloth. Have enough gift cards or tags with writing space on the back for everyone in the group. Have a Bible Dictionary handy. Choose some background music for the 'Steps' section. Provide the words and music of 'I cannot tell why he, whom angels worship' for the 'Surrender' section.

Starter

Place the table display in full view, if it isn't already.

Leader   Deserts are not very hospitable places, and yet there is a great tradition of hospitality in the desert. Listen to this story of Abraham as one example of desert hospitality.

Ask someone to read Genesis 18:1-15.

Leader   The author of 'Hebrews' may have had that story in mind when he urged the early Christians to show hospitality to strangers because some who have done so have entertained angels unawares (Hebrews 13:2). But sometimes it is those who practise hospitality who are the angels – ministering angels (see Matthew 4:11).

Contemplation

Someone lights the candle and/or incense.

24

Leader Lent is not just about giving things up; it's about giving them away. In fact it is about giving ourselves. We are stripped of inessentials in order that we may get in touch with what is truly essential, and then we share this.

Reader Only three things last for ever: faith, hope and love, and the greatest of these is love (1 Corinthians 13:13).

Leader Fourth century desert Christians fasted from fashion, foods and frivolity, yet when a visitor came a long distance on foot they gave the visitor their best meal and attention. Hospitality was second only to prayer as a rule of the desert.

Reader This week we journey with Jesus during his last few days, when so many deserted him. We learn how, when he was entering a desert of pain and doom, an ordinary household nourished him. Their hospitality took the form of doing something beautiful for him.

Scripture

John 12:1-8

Ask someone to read the passage aloud.

Ask the members of the group to share what they have found in their own study of this passage and prompt them by asking the following questions:

Leader What do you know about Bethany? *(Augment their answers, if necessary, by reading information from a Bible Dictionary.)*

What do you know about Mary, Martha and Lazarus? *(Again use a Bible Dictionary, if necessary.)*

From what we are told in John's Gospel about the days before and after this home gathering (the raising of Lazarus, the plot to kill Jesus, the plot to kill Lazarus, the entry into Jerusalem and all the events of Holy Week) what do you think would have been in Jesus' mind during this meal?

Sifting

Imagine what other people present might have been thinking – Martha, Lazarus, Judas Iscariot, Mary. *(Divide into four groups to discuss one of these characters each.)*

Is it possible that when Jesus, a few days later, washed his disciples' feet, he was thinking of what Mary had done for him in Bethany?

Steps

Play some appropriate background music quietly.

Leader   Jesus was weary from the pressures in the city, as he had been weary on his journey through Samaria when he sat by Jacob's well and asked the Samaritan woman for a drink (John 4:6,7); and as he had been weary after being tested in the desert. Ministering angels had come to him then, but in Bethany it was Mary (and Martha) who were his ministering angels.

Reader   Mary had an intimation that Jesus carried a huge burden of suffering and foreboding. That is why she had purchased expensive perfumed embalming oil and felt she needed to use it now, before Jesus' death, as a prophetic act of tender loving care. She did something beautiful for God.

Reader   We, too, can do something beautiful for God. From early times Christians gave gifts to needy people as one way of doing this. Almsgiving is important for Christians as well as Muslims. But Mary's gift was special, personal; it had much thought and love behind it. Now, in the stillness, I invite you to think of some act of love to Jesus that *you* can make. It may be in the form of a gift of time, treasure or talent directly to God, or to someone in need. When you are ready, take a gift tag, and write on it what you have decided to do, and then place the tag, with your writing face downwards, near the candle on the table. When you leave, you may take it with you. It is your secret gift.

Surrender

Sing the first two verses of 'I cannot tell, why he whom angels worship'.

Reader We mourn a life of such goodness, cut down in its flower.

We mourn for a people who forfeited the flowering of their destiny.

We mourn for a planet which rejected its Maker.

We mourn for ourselves, who languish alone and lost.

All Lord, we offer you our tears, our memories, our tenderness, our faith.

Reader As the rising incense (candle flame) speaks of your presence, may our hearts always rise to you in adoration.

All We offer ourselves to you in love and praise.

Reader As myrrh spreads the fragrance of perfume,

may the offering of our lives be fragrant to you.

All Lord, we offer ourselves to you in love and praise. Amen.

There may be refreshments, conversation or silence.

Ask the group members to study **Luke 22:39-46** *and* **Matthew 27:45-54** *at home in preparation for the next session.*

THE GARDEN OF PRAYER AND THE HILL OF PAIN

Preparations

You will need a plain cross (the more it looks like a tree, the better) and a picture of Jesus in Gethsemane. Have pencils and paper ready for the 'Starter' and 'Steps' sections, and have scissors, pieces of card and pins to give out for the 'Surrender' section.

Starter

Leader   Write down words which sum up the feelings you usually associate with Holy Week. Share your lists with the group.

Contemplation

Place the cross and the picture where they can be seen by all.

Leader   In this session we shall be thinking of Jesus' last hours on the cross and his preparation for them in the Garden. All that he had lived for was coming to its final climax.

First, let's recall how on Sunday the crowds cheered as Jesus rode on a donkey into Jerusalem; how during the next days he taught in the temple, preparing his followers to face what was to come. In the evenings he returned the two miles to Martha and Mary's home where he could relax with friends.

Then he was back in the city to share a last Passover supper with his friends. This was followed by betrayal, false accusations in clandestine courts through the night, whipping and the carrying of his heavy wooden cross on which he was nailed on Friday, and on which he died.

First we are with him after the Passover meal in the Garden of Gethsemane.

The leader reads Luke 22:39-46.

Leader   Imagine how Jesus would be feeling as he prayed in Gethsemane.

Allow about a minute for this.

Leader   Imagine how the disciples who were with him in the Garden would be feeling.

Allow a similar time for this.

Leader   Jesus was wide awake, but the disciples fell asleep. Contrast this with the story of the storm on the lake when the disciples panicked and Jesus slept.

'Not my will but yours be done.'

Imagine this place is the Garden of Gethsemane.
Walk to any spot inside or outside that is available to us.
Kneel down and keep repeating to yourself:

'Your will, not mine be done.'

After several minutes return in silence and share your thoughts if you wish.

Scripture

Matthew 27:45-54

Ask someone to read the passage aloud.

Invite the group to share the results of their study of this passage.

Leader   What did Jesus' pain on the cross consist of – physically, mentally, emotionally, spiritually?
When he cried out, 'My God, my God, why have you forsaken me?' he seemed to have lost his sense of the

presence of God. Was this the worst of his pains on the cross?

What makes us believe that God wasn't really absent on Good Friday?

Sifting

Leader   Have you ever had the feeling of God's absence in your own life? Do you now think that God was *really* absent at that time? If not, what has made you change your mind?

As the women looked from a distance *(verses 55, 56)* what pains do you think *they* were suffering?

Steps

Distribute the pieces of paper to every member of the group.

Ask them to think of experiences of physical, mental, emotional or spiritual pain in their lives which made them weep for others or for God.

Invite them to write some of them down on the pieces of paper and place them by the cross. Music of Christ's Passion may be played quietly while this is done.

Reader   Lord, we bring physical pains to you, who suffered pain for us.

All   Lord, strengthen and heal us all.

Reader   Lord, we bring mental pains to you, who suffered pain for us.

All   Lord, strengthen and heal us all.

Reader   Lord, we bring emotional pains to you, who suffered pain for us.

All   Lord, strengthen and heal us all.

Reader   Lord, we bring spiritual pains to you, who suffered pain for us.

All   Lord, strengthen and heal us all. Amen.

Surrender

Sing or listen to a song about Christ's Passion, such as 'When I survey the wondrous cross', or use the following:

> When my love to Christ grows weak,
>   when for deeper faith I seek,
>   then in thought I go to thee,
>   Garden of Gethsemane.
>
> There I walk amid the shades,
>   while the lingering twilight fades,
>   see that suffering, friendless one,
>   weeping, praying there alone.
>
> When my love for man grows weak,
>   when for stronger faith I seek,
>   hill of Calvary, I go
>   to thy scenes of fear and woe.
>
> There behold his agony,
>   suffered on the bitter tree;
>   see his anguish, see his faith,
>   love triumphant still in death.
>
> Then to life I turn again,
>   learning all the worth of pain,
>   learning all the might that lies
>   in a full self-sacrifice.
>
> And I praise with firmer faith
>   Christ, who vanquished pain and death;
>   and to Christ enthroned above
>   raise my song of selfless love.
>
> *(J. R. Wreford, 1800-81) alt.*

Leader   Jesus, one of the two thieves who were dying each side of you asked you to have mercy on him when he came into your kingdom; we, too, ask for mercy.

31

All   Lord Jesus Christ, truly God, truly human, have mercy upon us.

Leader You are nailed to a tree, the sun hides its face, and all creation weeps.

All   Lord Jesus Christ, truly God, truly human, have mercy upon us.

Leader A grave will hold you, who holds creation in your hands.

All   Lord Jesus Christ, truly God, truly human, have mercy upon us.

Leader Women will go to your tomb and place spices of devotion.

All   Lord Jesus Christ, truly God, truly human, have mercy upon us.

Leader But the Tree of Death will be turned into the Tree of Life Everlasting.

All   Lord Jesus Christ, truly God, truly human, have mercy upon us.

Each person cuts out the shape of a tree and pins it to another person.

Leader Let us touch the Tree of the Cross
that will pour out immortality on the world
like a new river from Paradise.

All   We place the tree upon which Christ was crucified
between us and each evil thing.

Leader O King of the Friday
whose limbs were stretched on the cross,
O Lord who did suffer
the bruises, the wounds, the loss.

All   Some fruit from the tree of your passion
fall this Easter on us.

There may be refreshments, conversation or silence.